To Cynthia
With
for

from

CW00734982

kkx

HELFORD

A RIVER AND SOME LANDSCAPES

First published in Great Britain in 2005

Copyright © Tom Cross 2005

*All rights reserved.   No part of this publication may be reproduced,
stored in a retrieval system, or transmitted in any form or by any
means without the prior permission of the copyright holder.*

British Library Cataloguing-in-Publication Data
A CIP record for this title is available from the British Library

ISBN 1 84114 436 3

HALSGROVE
Halsgrove House
Lower Moor Way
Tiverton, Devon EX16 6SS
Tel: 01884 243242
Fax: 01884 243325
email: sales@halsgrove.com
website: www.halsgrove.com

Printed and bound by D'Auria Industrie Grafiche Spa, Italy

This book is dedicated to David and Carol

HELFORD

A RIVER AND SOME LANDSCAPES

TOM CROSS

HALSGROVE

LOCATION MAP

CONTENTS

Merthen Woods 2000
Oil on canvas 82 x 102 cm

CHAPTER ONE
THE RIVER

In 1984, writing in the Southern United States, I described the landscape in which I lived.

The river is the Helford River which flows to the sea near my home in Cornwall, England, in these last miles the main streams join to flow between deeply overhanging banks of scrub oak and rounded pasture land, through miles of tidal channels and mud creeks before it broadens into the gulf stream, still warm from its long passage across the Atlantic, a bond between Britain and the United States. (Introduction to the exhibition 'A River and Some Landscapes', Simons Centre for the Arts, Charleston, South Carolina, May 1984).

The Helford River has mystery and many ancient associations with pirates and wreckers, fishermen and tinners. Frenchman's Creek is one of its hidden delights. It also has great variety and unspoilt beauty, seen best from a boat or glimpsed from overgrown footpaths, constantly changing with the hour of the day or the movement of the seasons. In the height of the summer its sun-flashed beaches are a quiet escape shared only by the patrolling herons or the distant yachtsman.

In recent years the river has become my principal subject for painting and I am daily aware of the changes of weather and of the seasons. In describing this landscape I am conscious not only of the forms of land and the reflecting surface of water but the interaction of tide, current and wind. To travel on the river by boat provides another dimension, the perspective changing as you move between headlands. To quote Peter Lanyon's description of Cornwall, it is 'a place where solids and fluids meet'. Living, as I do on the north bank of the river, many of my paintings are to do with the area in which I live, Port Navas and it's is surroundings, including Calamansac Woods, where I walk my dog. It is a magic place where the river shines between the trees.

This is not intended to be a comprehensive catalogue of my painting, rather a series of comments and observations on my work as it has developed over the years. It includes statements made in connection with some of the exhibitions that I have taken part in as well as descriptions of the river by others who knew it well. For almost twenty years I have lived beside this river, my studio was once a cottage called 'Tire Me Out' and we are told that a man brought up his family of ten children in it. In front of it is the cider press we dug out of the ground, evidence of the time when each cottage made their own cider, grew their own vegetables and ate the oysters from the river.

Painting is a continuous process. It is done every day and over a period of time styles and subjects change and develop. In a sense the same thing is always being looked for and one searches for the ability to put down thoughts and feelings simply and clearly. But there are many ways of achieving this. If I look over a lifetime as a painter I can see the way in which the pattern of my work has changed. I can also recognise certain fixed points, signposts across the years.

Although I am not a topographical artist, wild and natural landscape has held a continuous attraction for me. My interest is not in detailed description of a place, rather I seek to explore the emotional aspects of landscape, affected by the varied conditions of wind and weather, the time of day and the whole experience. Coupled with this is the need to define the structure of the landscape, which often means simplifying it in order to understand it better.

The Helford River looks to its ancient past. The sheltered position and ease of communication by water brought many early settlements to the edges of the river. In medieval times a number of religious communities grew up along the estuary. Farms and small hamlets developed as agriculture intensified. Oysters and other shellfish were cultivated and most of the hamlets built large fish cellars where fish were packed and equipment for the fishing was stored. Trade flourished, centred upon the ports of Helford, Gweek and Gillan. Tin, coal and timber were carried to the villages and to the large houses that were built along the river.

The river has retained a balance between its earlier development for industrial purposes, the transportation of granite, fishing and farming and its present use as a centre for sailing and other water sports. The large number of moorings for summer use in the lower estuary of the river contrasts with the remoteness and tranquillity in the upper reaches above Port Navas.

In considering this book I made certain decisions. The first was to write it in the first person. These notes are a commentary on my work over the years and they include various statements made in connection with exhibitions. With such material it would be foolish to hide behind such conventions as 'the author' or to pretend that these notes were written by some anonymous and invisible other.

The second important decision was to assemble these ideas in reverse chronological order. This was done to give prominence to my more recent work, much of which has been based upon the Helford River. I am also intrigued by the thought that I am the product of the various influences that have gone before, some of these are powerful and these factors help to form my work as an artist. The many influences that have gone before form part of one's personal history.

The book falls into three distinct parts: Chapters 1 to 3 are largely a description of the geography, history and natural history of the Helford. All of these are factors that affect my current painting. Two chapters follow, which describe the general environment in which I work. The remainder of the book is largely autobiographical and discusses the earlier influences on my painting and some of the by-ways that I have explored.

This river has attracted many artists and writers. Lady Clara Vyvyan, the second wife of Sir Courtney Vyvyan of Trelowarren was a writer who knew the river intimately. She asks the question 'What is the Helford River?'

Well, to begin with, there is all the river, that tract of country drained by the Helford and its tributaries; a land of secret valleys where flowers bloom all through the winter, of snipe-haunted moorland that lies open to the sky and is overgrown with the rampant Cornish heather, of hillside gashed by granite quarries and crowned by granite boulders piled like the bricks of a child on many a crest of land; of woodland where oak saplings interlace their boughs in their struggle towards the light, of woodland where ancestral beech stand in groups and every stem is like a monolith remaining in the proud isolation from its neighbours; a land of ancient manor houses, of low cottages, some of which retain their beauty, of thatched roof and white-washed walls, of irregular hamlet and village and grey church towers; of strange pylons standing on their concreted bases and towering towards the sky with deserted Nissen huts beneath them; a land full of gardens, wild flowers, fungi, lichen, ferns.

C J Vyvyan. *The Helford River.* Peter Owen Ltd. London 1956

HELFORD – A RIVER AND SOME LANDSCAPES

The Helford River also held a special attraction for Daphne du Maurier. In July 1932 she and 'Boy' Browning, then a Major in the Grenadier Guards, were married in the little church at Lanteglos near Fowey. The wedding took place in the early morning so that the couple could catch the early tide. Daphne du Maurier's biographer Margaret Forester described the day:

Afterwards there was a breakfast at Ferryside before the bride and groom changed into their beloved old clothes, jumped into Ygdrasil, and set off for the open sea. They sailed to the Helford river and moored for the night in Frenchman's Creek, where on a summer's evening the trees are so dense it seems a mysterious place. They were hidden away, just as Daphne wanted. The only sounds were the slapping of the slow running water against the side of the boat and the screeching of the seagulls. It struck her as extraordinary that she was here at all, that her life had changed so dramatically within the space of three months. She had made her mind up so quickly, perfectly realizing how terrifying this was, but excited to be following her own instinct. She was proud of her own daring and proud of her husband. The deed was done. The stars glittered through the thick overhead canopy of leaves hanging over the boat, and the slim crescent of a new moon wavered above. It was all quite perfect.

Margaret Forester. *Daphne du Maurier*. Chatto & Windus, London 1993.

Oyster Quay 1997
Oil on canvas 51 x 61 cm

Merthen Woods 2004
Oil on canvas 71 x 71 cm

West Wind 2002
Watercolour 22 x 31 cm

Winter on Helford River 2002
Watercolour 25 x 38 cm

Oyster Quay 1995
Oil on canvas 106 x 122 cm

Moorings 2004
Oil on canvas 66 x 71 cm

Low Tide, Helford River 2000
Oil on canvas 92 x 159 cm

Abraham's Bosom 2001
Oil on canvas 50 x 50 cm

West Beach 2004
Oil on canvas 56 x 124 cm

CHAPTER TWO

THE MOUTH OF THE RIVER

The Helford Estuary is the most southerly in Britain. The length of the river to Gweek, the furthest point inland, is just over six miles. There is a great deal of variety along its length. In its earlier stages the river twists and turns through numerous tidal creeks and is fed by many small streams. As the river reaches the sea the surrounding landscape is of steep cliffs, backed by open grassland.

The Helford is a tidal river along its length from the headlands of Dennis Head and Toll Point to the little village of Gweek with its two bridges. The tide flows most quickly at Groyne Point the halfway mark along the length of the river. Here the river is joined by the major tributary, Polwheveral Creek, which rises near Constantine to the north. At high tide there is deep blue water here; but when the tide is low the river is reduced to two narrow, fast-flowing streams many feet below the mud flats where birds congregate to feed.

The seaward entrance to the Helford River is guarded to the north by Rosemullion Head, a stretch of broken coast with platforms of sea-washed rock that are the home to many marine creatures. From Toll Point, below the church, are the most extensive views of the river and the sea beyond. Offshore from Rosemullion Head are the line of fearsome rocks known as 'The Gedges' also called 'August Rock' which show at low tide. The old church of Mawnan sits beside the coastal foot-path on high ground which was the oval site of an ancient earthwork. It is a landmark for vessels entering the river from the south-east; when it is visually aligned with Nare Point an incoming boat will clear the Manacles Rocks.

to Lizard and the Manacles.   3 Oct 98

The entrance to the river from the south is protected by Nare Point an area of reefs and rock pools backed by low rolling hills. This was the scene of the wreck of the four-masted sailing ship the *Bay of Panama* that was driven aground on the night of a terrible storm in November 1891.

Branching off the mouth of the Helford just north of Nare Point is Gillan Creek, a wide stretch of water protected by low hills. A narrow lane runs alongside these quiet reaches to the village of Gillan, now a tiny harbour with a mixture of pleasure boats and fishing craft. In earlier times a cliff castle stood at the entrance to this approach from the sea, and Bronze Age barrows and ancient artefacts have been found. The church at Gillan dates from the twelfth century when this was a busy port, exporting fish, fish oil and salt. It later shipped tin from the small mines on The Lizard. Nearby is the even smaller village of Carne which was once the site of a busy mill.

Dennis Head stands above Gillan Creek in a commanding position overlooking both sea and countryside. The name is a corruption from the Cornish 'Dinas' meaning castle or fort and the remains of a large Iron Age castle stand on this headland. During the Civil War this became one of the last Royalist strongholds in Cornwall. Another of the tiny villages that lie like a necklace around this magical creek is St Anthony-in-Meneage. The church of St Anthony was built of stone brought from Normandy, possibly by invaders from that area. This ancient church is built on the beach and sits beside the hulls of yachts drawn up for winter storage, their masts as high as the church tower. Arthur Mee described St Anthony as 'A churchyard, which is a garden, by the water's edge with flowers shrubs and trees.' In the churchyard is a moving memorial to Crispin Rushworth Lund, who was murdered in the West Indies, following the accidental drowning of his young child. The inscription on his headstone reads:

From Otter Lodge
Feburary 1995

A Tree, reflection to be darker
/ Water lighter.

> *Lois and Crispin Rushworth Lund*
> *2.10.87 – 22.3.90   6.1.50 – 21.5.90*
> *Darling Little Lois*
> *An arrow drawn to water*
> *And taken by water*
> *Our Love forever*
> *Mummy Daddy Alice*
> *Darling Crispin*
> *So cruelly shot down*
> *Sleep peacefully with Lois*
> *And watch over us*
> *Belinda and Alice and your many friends.*

This valley widens out in to a shallow tidal creek, noted for the profusion of cockle beds which are traditionally harvested once a year by local people, a practice known as 'trigging'. This occurs on Good Fridays, which often coincides with the lowest tides of the month. At the head of the creek

is the village of Manaccan, a cluster of whitewashed cottages with an ancient thatched public house among them, appropriately called The New Inn. The church of St Manaccan has a 200-year-old fig tree growing out of the southern wall. Away from the coast, in a surrealist landscape of boulders and gorse, the flat landscape of The Lizard peninsula is dominated by the great dishes of the radio aerials of Goonhilly Downs.

Around the narrows of the river at Helford Passage lie the main centres of population, between Port Navas to the north and Helford village to the south. Behind the river a network of narrow lanes has developed from the farm tracks linking the various hamlets, but the most direct way to travel around the river is by boat. Yachts and pleasure boats of all types congregate around the village of Helford, which stands in a wooded valley about halfway along the southern bank of the river. This is the oldest settlement on the Helford river and an early centre of marine activity and boat building. As these industries began to decline so the tourist industry developed. In the mid twentieth century the smaller cottages, once occupied by local people engaged in fishing and farming, became holiday lets, and a number of the larger country houses were turned into hotels. This picturesque village was described unflatteringly by John Betjeman as 'much resorted to by yachtsmen and beardies.' (*A Shell Guide to Cornwall*. Faber & Faber 1964).

Since medieval times the two shores of the river have been joined by a ferry which crosses from Helford to Helford Passage. This is now officially part of the Cornish coastal footpath. There is no continuous footpath along the upper reaches of the river, a characteristic that gives the Helford its distinctive charm, and the upper reaches their remoteness. The old school house at Durgan is a prominent nineteenth-century building which replaced an earlier fish cellar.

The two great gardens, Trebah and Glendurgan, which lie alongside each other are a special delight. They were both laid out in the 1840s for members of the Fox family who were then the most important of the Falmouth shipping magnates. The garden at Trebah was first created by Charles Fox who travelled widely and imported rare and exotic plants from all over the world. The great screens of pines which gave protection to the two gardens were planted by him.

Each of the gardens have different characteristics. Glendurgan, which is now under the management of the National Trust, is a flattened horseshoe, wide and somewhat shallow, the tall trees well away to the sides. In the central part is a maze of considerable complexity. At Trebah the garden is in a steeply-wooded ravine dropping to the beach below. The finest trees, some as much as 150 years old, form a narrow perspective down which the silver ribbon of the river is always in sight. Trebah is also remarkable for the giant rhododendrons and the tall Chusan palms. It has a large collection of tree ferns, some as much as 100 years old brought from New Zealand as part of a cargo that replenished many of the great Cornish gardens.

Trebah garden was at its heyday in Edwardian times and it was developed under various owners until the Second World War when the house was sold and the estate broken up. In the period leading up to the Normandy landings in the Second World War, Trebah was again an important centre of activity. It was here that military train-ing took place and American tanks and lorries were embarked on landing craft for the D-Day invasion. In 1948 the old eighteenth-century house was destroyed by fire and from that time, the gardens were sadly neglected. In 1980 the Hibbert family bought Trebah and a massive programme of restoration and planting began. In 1987 the gardens were opened to the public and three years later, by the generosity of the

Abrahams Bosom.   August 2000

Hibbert family, the house and garden became the Trebah Garden Trust, thus saving it for future generations.

The sheltered pool known locally as Abraham's Bosom connects the main river with Port Navas Creek and provides safe mooring for boats and a nursery area for the novice sailor. Nearby the sandy shore of Bar Beach dries out at the lowest tides and reveals a rich mixture of sand and mud. Upstream from the point of Pedn Billy is a large area of quiet water also shown on the charts as 'mud'. At low tide it is the home for the many wading birds, between tides it is a sun-filled beach known as West Beach and backed by the oak woods of Calamansac.

The village of Port Navas, previously known as Cove, is now a largely residential creek-side village but until recently it was a centre for heavy industry. At the beginning of the twentieth century Port Navas was a scene of great activity with cranes and derricks loading large blocks of granite brought down by heavy horses from the Constantine quarries. At Port Navas it was loaded on to coastal vessels taking it to London and beyond. These blocks can be seen in old photographs, sitting on the quay in piles some 40 or 50 feet in height, awaiting shipment.

Port Navas is also the home of the Duchy Oyster Farm where oysters and mussels are sent off around the country. Since 1982, when the greater part of the oyster population was wiped out by disease, the oyster farm has acted as a packing and cleaning centre for oysters, However the presence of the Oysterage, managed by generations of the Hodges family, has helped to keep the upper reaches of the Helford River unspoilt.

Abrahams Bosom. Sat 25 April 96. Tidal outflow.

Abraham's Bosom 2000
Oil on canvas 46 x 56 cm

Dennis Head 2000
Oil on canvas 41 x 51 cm

St Anthony 2000
Oil on canvas 92 x 102 cm

The Church of St Anthony 1990
Ink and Wash

Bosloe, 1997
Watercolour 76.5 x 54 cm

Old Quay, Frenchman's Creek 2000
Oil on canvas 47 x 57 cm

Dennis Head 2004
Oil on canvas 76 x 102 cm

CHAPTER THREE
THE UPPER RIVER

In contrast to the busy villages and creeks of the lower river the upper parts of the river remain remarkably tranquil and remote. These upper creeks are heavily wooded with large areas described as 'ancient', that is more than 200 years old. Access is very limited. Apart from the occasional boathouse there are few buildings, no roads and hardly any footpaths until the crossing at Gweek.

Clara Vyvyan, writing in the period before and after the Second World War, offers an explanation as to why the upper reaches of the Helford are so unspoilt. She believed that this was because of the attitudes of a small number of landowners on both sides of the river. She writes of the 'old landlord who played a large part in saving the peace and beauty of the Helford River over many years'. This was her husband Sir Courtney Vyvyan; he had ownership of the woods, beaches, fields and farms extending along many miles of the southern shore of the Helford from Gweek to Frenchman's Creek. He was of the opinion that the beauty of this land must be kept inviolate and that no building should be permitted along the shores of the river. He would refuse to sell any plot on the margin of the river for building purposes. As Clara Vyvyan explains 'on his property he would not permit the erection of any building that would break into the quietness of these fields and slopes of bracken and on the reflections of those clouds and trees, on the solitude of those herons, ducks, gulls and curlews'.

On the opposite bank the Warington Smyth family, well known for designing and building boats and for yacht racing, similarly protected the seclusion of the upper reaches. There was tacit agreement with 'the old landlord' that while he preserved the sanctities of the southern shore they would keep intact their great promontory of oak woods on the northern side.

The two great houses of Trelowarren and Merthen lie on opposite sides of the upper river; the river was not a dividing line here. The name of the Vyvyan family and their home Trelowarren has been associated with the Helford since ancient times. Members of the family were known to be in the area in the fourteenth century when their reputation included wrecking and other nefarious deeds. The manor house of Trelowarren, built in the sixteenth century to replace an earlier dwelling, is set back from the river in a sheltered hollow protected from the north and west by tall trees. At the time of the Civil War it was a centre of Royalist support.

The Chapel, Trelowarren.

The owner of Trelowarren in the period between the wars was Sir Courtney Vyvyan who died in 1940; his first wife had died in 1928. Lady Clara Vyvyan, his second wife, struggled to maintain the great house during the Second World War and was able to establish a successful market garden on the estate. In recent times the main part of the house and the old chapel has become a Christian Fellowship, with the family living in the wings.

From about 1644 Merthen was part of the Trelowarren estate and very ancient as a site. In antiquity the manor was a royal one, the Saxon princes looked upon it as one of their most valuable possessions and it is recorded that King Edward the Confessor passed it to King Harold and then to William the Conqueror.

The Reskymer family built the Manor of Merthen on the site of an older house, which had become a ruin. The Manor House is a grey granite building with a massive porch and an arched doorway, ornamented with stylised fan leaves and a room above. The date 1575 is inscribed over the porch; on one side is a hall and on the other a parlour. In the seventeenth century the Manor became the property of Sir Francis Vyvyan, knight of Trelowarren, whose son Richard was created a Baronet by Charles I.

Merthen Manor.

This royal connection gave the lords of the Manor of Merthen the right to fish in the river and the oyster beds. They had rights to what is called 'head fish' in the upper reaches of the river including porpoise, dolphin, tonnny and thorpole ('a great bare-bellied fish') as well as the oysters. They also had rights over wrecks in the river. There were often law suits over these matters and at one point in the nineteenth century, almost a riot, when Sir Richard Vyvyan called in an armed cutter from Plymouth to protect his oysters.

In the 1930s there was a huge sale of Vyvyan properties and most of the local tenant farmers took the opportunity to buy their farms. It was at this time that much of the woodland was bought by members of the Warington Smyth family. The sale catalogue even included Merthen Manor, but this did not sell and Lady Clara Vyvyan later bought it and gave it to the present owners and it remains in the Vyvyan family.

The river at Polwheveral from the ancient site.   9 May 05

Polwheveral Creek is the largest of the creeks on the Helford, surrounded by farmland and scattered groups of cottages, some of which are of considerable age. The woods at Polwheveral were planted in the eighteenth century to provide fuel for the smelters and charcoal burners. A tucking and fulling mill at Polwheveral was used for cloth finishing. At low tide this creek dries to mud and provides a rich feeding ground for a large variety of bird life.

Enclosed and mysterious, Frenchman's Creek has a powerful emotional message. No roads touch it; only a narrow footpath runs along the shoreline. The reputation of mystery that surrounds it is due to the remoteness and the silence that is so evident. It is a world given wholly to the birds; trees almost meet overhead and at low tide a narrow channel runs between deep mud banks revealing the skeletal remains of oak trees that have been washed into the eroding stream. For the painter these predatory shapes of meeting branches become a series of beak shapes that peck across the river, and the dead and decaying trees have a surreal malevolence.

The previous importance of Frenchman's Creek as an active marine area is illustrated by the fact that this remote creek had four quays, three of which still survive. In earlier times this narrow stretch

of water provided a perfect hideaway for smuggling. This less savoury reputation became popularly known when it was the subject for Daphne du Maurier's first major novel *Frenchman's Creek* published in 1941.

At the entrance to Frenchman's Creek is a wooden house recently acquired by the National Trust, repaired and re-named as 'Powder' in memory of the man who built it. With his own efforts and mostly with his own hands, he created this house and studio for himself and his wife. He built an enclave around this large and comfortable building as well as several smaller buildings dotted about the surrounding land, including a summerhouse overhanging the water, a sleeping cabin and a dwelling for the man who helped him.

In addition to being a builder, boat builder and fisherman, Powder, whose real name was P.C. Thurburn, was also a skilful artist. He painted his memories of his early days at sea, as a crew member in square-rigged sailing boats making long passages in blue water. He painted the boats working on the Helford River and the landscape. Painting was interspersed with his love of deep-sea fishing. He did

not exhibit his work in his lifetime but his paintings found their way into many private collections in the area, mostly paid for by a bottle of whisky or rum.

As far as it was possible he was completely self-contained. In his later years he became more reclusive and his reputation was of the solitary, with simple tastes. After the death of his wife he lived an isolated existence without electricity or telephone, fishing from boats that he built himself. He tanned his own sails and waterproofed his own oilskins and lived for more than fifty years in this self-imposed hermitage.

A number of quays lie along the Helford River, built to serve the villages and great houses for the transport of coal, wood, building materials and other essentials. On the south side the slopes are less wooded and the river is fringed with pastureland but there are small woods overlooking Tremayne boathouse and the three creeks Ponsantuel, Vellan Tremayne and Frenchman's Pill. Bishop's Quay, the home of the Kirby family, was and still is a fishing quay. At Gweek two streams enter the river, each under its own bridge, and five roads converge from Constantine, Falmouth, Helston, St Keverne and The Lizard.

Scotts Quay.

Sir Richard Vyvyan built Tremayne Quay in the mid nineteenth century for a cruise planned along the Cornish coast for Queen Victoria and Prince Albert. However, because of bad weather the cruise was cancelled and the visit never took place. The house Tremayne acted as a dower house for Trelowarren. At the head of Polwheveral is Scott's Quay, built in the nineteenth century for shipping granite.

The main course of the river begins at Gweek, which is the first bridging point between the two banks. Gweek was first settled in the twelfth century and became a trading post for Helston and the surrounding area. In the eighteenth and nineteenth centuries Gweek became a major centre of trade, with boats from Scandinavia, Germany, Holland and Ireland tied up along side the busy quays. It was possible to buy a ticket in Gweek for a passage on one of the emigrant boats to Boston and other ports in the USA. Its long quays and wharves now provide boatyard facilities for the repair and maintenance of yachts and shipping.

Gweek is also the home of the National Seal Sanctuary, a wildlife centre where injured seals are treated and returned to the wild. Ken Jones, a retired miner and his wife Mary, started this in 1960. Initially a small-scale venture, the Sanctuary now acts as a hospital and rehabilitation unit for injured seals brought here from a wide area.

Groyne Point 2004
Oil on canvas 71 x 82 cm

Merthen Quay 1995
Watercolour 35 x 53 cm

Gweek Quay, Helford River 1998
Watercolour 51 x 54 cm

Gweek Quay 1989
Watercolour 24 x 30 cm

Frenchman's Creek 2, 1997
Oil on canvas 41 x 51 cm

Frenchman's Creek 1997
Oil on canvas 56 x 66 cm

Polwheveral Creek 1996
Oil on board 102 x 22 cm

Scott's Quay, Low Tide 2004
Oil on canvas 61 x 76 cm

Scott's Quay 1997
Oil on canvas 56 x 76 cm

CHAPTER FOUR

WIND AND WATER INTO ABSTRACT SHAPE

The brilliant light of Cornwall, the almost Mediterranean blue of the sea and the formation of rock and cliff have had a powerful effect on my work. These produced changes, most noticeable over a period of some three years from 1975 to 1978 and marked by my move from the centre of England to its most extreme westerly tip.

In a series of watercolours and gouaches the formal images of earlier paintings were replaced by work based more on observation. In describing different aspects of the river landscape I am conscious not only of the forms of the land and the reflecting surfaces of water, but the action of tides, current and wind which make up the totality of experience. These must be translated into shape and colour. They are no longer totally abstract but they share with the earlier images a preoccupation for a framework or structure, which underlies appearance.

My painting up to this time had been largely concerned with architectural space, the buildings and spaces in which we live. These alternated with drawings and paintings of landscape, mostly the landscape of Wales and Italy. Many of these were not painted on the spot – there is rarely time or privacy to work on complex paintings out of doors, but studies were made from nature, usually in ink or pencil reinforced with watercolour. In the studio they would be given more solid form as oil paintings or as larger gouache or watercolour paintings.

Whatever the starting point, these largely abstract images usually refer to something seen in landscape and are an attempt to recapture that experience. In this respect it is

little different from working with a series of abstract shapes. The receding planes must be flattened and the elements of design made to work as a harmonious whole. At first these drawings were little more than diagrams, skeletal arrangements with the features of the river landscape represented by simplified shapes of hill, headland, tide and current. The next stage was a group of paintings in which the forms of land and water were simplified but in a less diagramatic way. Examples of these are paintings such as 'River Turning' of 1988 or 'River Rising' of 1987. Here the river is shown in turbulent mood, the sometimes violent forms held in check by flattened shapes and strong colour.

Abstraction was an important element in all of these paintings. By this I mean a simplicity of form, attention to proportion and balance. This also meant a reduction in direct references to observed nature. This was not the calculated and precise abstraction practised by some of the leading artists of the earlier part of the twentieth century such as the purist abstraction of Mondrian or the precision of the pre-war abstractions of Ben Nicholson. In my case the images were more roughly drawn with colour applied in flattened areas.

By detaching the painting from accurate observation it became possible to find greater freedom in the sweep of shape and the interaction of line. Above all colour, which became an element in it's own right. The use of strong colour has long been a major component in modern painting. In 1888 Paul Gauguin instructed his follower Paul Serusier in the use of colour as an equivalent for sensation. Seated in front of a landscape Gauguin demanded: 'How do you see that tree? It's green? Then choose the most beautiful green in your palette – and this shadow? It's more like blue? Do not be afraid to paint it with the purest blue possible.' (*L'Influence de Paul Gauguin*. L'Occident 1903).

After moving to Cornwall I began to find subjects in the Helford area, following a summer spent in a cottage at Calamansac, overlooking the river. I was looking for a way in which the fleeting movement of wind and water could be incorporated into paintings, together with such intangibles as the tidal rise and fall and the changing effects of light.

As the series developed and I obtained more information from observation, these arrangements took on a more substantial form. This was not intended to be a deliberate advance towards naturalistic painting. The intention is to create a balance between naturalism and abstraction, one enriching the other. Each part of the painting is true as shape and colour yet it also reveals the characteristics of landscape.

A group of paintings had the general title 'West Beach'. This is the local name for a part of the river's edge above Port Navas and opposite to Frenchman's Creek. It is fed by the main stream of the river

From West Beach

and by Polwheveral Creek, the largest of the Helford creeks. This extensive sheet of water has many changes of appearance during each day. At low water the western edge becomes an opaque surface of drying mud in which a multitude of seabirds search for food, guarded by the shrill call of the curlew. At high tide the shallow waters respond to the wind funnelling down the river and reflect the movement of cloud and aerial current. The West Beach paintings come from studies made at different times of day. They are not topographical in the sense that they are intended to give detailed information about one particular place, rather they generalise the feeling of the river landscape.

Photograph by Eric Roberts

The artist at work.

Drawings of Helford Subjects 1998
Ink on Paper

Reach of the River 1987
Watercolour

Riverbank 1995
Oil on canvas 51 x 54 cm

Winter Evening 1990
Gouache 53 x 72 cm

West Beach 3, 1989
Gouache 28 x 28 cm

West Beach 1992
Gouache 54 x 62 cm

West Beach, Summer 1990
Gouache 53 x 72 cm

CHAPTER FIVE

THE SEQUENCE OF WORK

I often take my boat out to do some drawing. Certain sites attract me and I visit them repeatedly, on foot or by boat. My house overlooks the river, I see it at all times of day, in gentle or stormy mood. The east–west alignment of the river gives a dramatic range from strongly lit subjects to the effects of backlighting. Working from landscape out of doors I mostly make small sketch drawings in pencil or watercolour. In the studio these become the basis of full-size drawings which contain the main elements of the design. The object is to keep as closely as possible to the original sensations of the place.

The real subject is the wind and water, the roughness of the terrain, the movement of the sun, the time of day and the march of the seasons. Many of these are intangible or ephemeral. For many artists in the twentieth century the solution to this problem lay in abstraction.

The St Ives artist John Wells put this dilemma most clearly. Writing to his friend Sven Berlin in 1945 Wells described the strong feelings that he tried to capture:

So all around the morning air and the sea's blue light, with points of diamond and the gorse incandescent beyond the trees, countless rocks ragged or round and of every colour, birds resting or flying and the sense of a multitude of creatures living out their minute lives... All of this is part of one's life and I want desperately to express it, not just what I see but what I feel about it... but how can one paint the warmth of the sun, the sound of the sea, the journey of a beetle across a rock, or thoughts of one's own whence and whither? That's one argument for abstraction. One absorbs all these feelings and ideas; if one is lucky they undergo an alchemistic transformation into gold and that is creative work.

Shortly after coming to Cornwall I became very involved with those members of the St Ives group that were still working in Cornwall, including John Wells. In 1984 I wrote a history of the artistic events that had taken place in this remarkable small town in the 1940s and 1950s. The title of the book, taken from the letter that I have just quoted, was *Painting the Warmth of the Sun*, published originally by Alison Hodge and Lutterworth Press in 1984, and latterly by Halsgrove.

In my own work an important stage in the process is the preparation of working drawings or cartoons. These are done on thin paper to the full size of the finished work, however large that will be, even for paintings two metres or more in length. These drawings help me to understand the space within the picture, the relative size of objects, placing and proportion and the abstract elements of the painting. When the drawing has been taken as far as possible it is transferred to the canvas or watercolour paper. The painting therefore begins with these essential ingredients in position. If, as often happens, the painting needs reworking, these full size drawings serve as a reminder to bring me back to my original purpose. They are not intended for exhibition or display.

It may sound as if the process is one of careful planning, however this sequence which sometimes involves extensive reworking, gives me an intimate knowledge of the subject. I also use fortuitous accident, such as the use of texture or resist in watercolour or over-painting in oil. My intention is

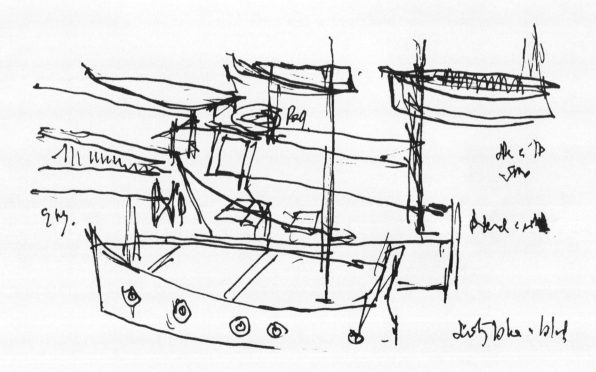

always to return to the first moment, to treasure the original impact of the place or idea. This may come after careful consideration or it may be produced in a moment by a swiftly drawn line, in extreme cases by literally throwing paint at the paper. Either judgement or emotional response may bring me back to that first sensation, there are no rules. The quality of the painting is judged by the feeling that comes through, one will know when it works and recognise it when it does.

I don't want my paintings to be flat; they should have some spatial depth. The shapes within the painting contain the space and the way the shape is held is very important to me. I am also interested in the geometry of perspective and the penetration of space made by colour, as in the painting 'A Path in Calamansac Woods'.

In one sense a painting is never complete, I usually stop because problems have been raised which are better dealt with in another painting. At that point I am pleased to see the painting leave the studio because it gives the opportunity to tackle something else.

Often the theme will rest on an idea, rather than a particular place. An example of this is a series of paintings which I have returned to over the years, under the title 'Headlands'. They arise from the sensation of moving on water in a small boat towards a distant horizon and passing along a series of coastal promontories. A characteristic of the north bank of the Helford is the oak woods that come down to the river. The river is seen through the trees, there are few footpaths and most of the woods are inaccessible to the public. It is here that the most ancient of the oak woods are found, naturally renewed over the centuries. In pictorial terms the distant landscape of the darkening river is glimpsed through a thin screen of trees. The light breeze moving over the surface of the water has it's own geometry. These produced a group of paintings based upon an idea rather than on observation under the title 'Last Leaves'.

Entrance to Gillan Creek 2004
Oil on canvas 76 x 102 cm

Drawing for Entrance to Gillan Creek 2004
Chalk on paper 76 x 102 cm

Evening Light 1988
Gouache 53 x 72 cm

Headlands 1983
Oil on canvas 1
152 x 101 cm

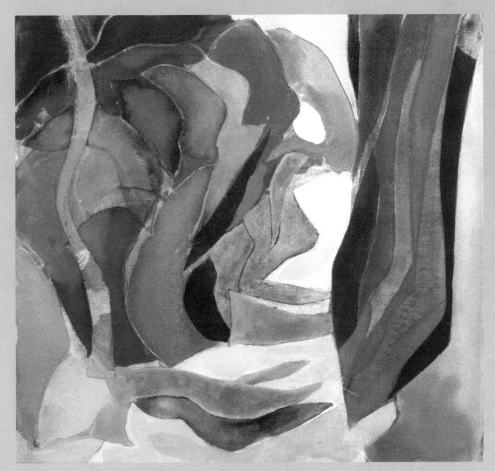

Path in Calamansac Woods 1987
Gouache 38 x 41 cm

Sketch for West Beach 1990
Gouache 18x 19cm

Sketch for West Beach, Winter Evening 1990
Watercolour 24 x 26 cm

West Beach,
Morning Light 1990
Gouache

Last Leaves 1993
Oil on canvas 191 x 122 cm

Calamansac Wood 1989
Gouache 37 x cm

River Landscape 1998
Watercolour 74 x 55 cm

Woodland 1999
Oil on canvas (4 panels) 46 x 124 cm

Calamansac Woods 2000
Oil on canvas 92 x 153 cm

CHAPTER SIX

THE MOVE TO CORNWALL

In 1976, with my family I moved to Cornwall to become Principal of Falmouth School of Art. Almost from the first the particular qualities of the Cornish landscape, its spectacular coastline and iridescent light, began to affect my work. My subjects were mostly located around the rivers. I lived in Falmouth overlooking the River Fal and the Carrick Roads with its constant stream of boats and shipping.

To what extent did running Falmouth School of Art interfere with painting? Well, it's very unpopular for the Principal to go down to his studio at 4 o'clock in the afternoon, but I thought that it was most important for the School as well as for myself to keep on painting. The problem of having a largely administrative job is that one cannot do as much practical art work as one would wish; ideas cannot be turned over with sufficient freedom.

Cornwall has been a magnet for artists for more than one hundred years. The Art School in Falmouth was a product of this attraction, a small but high-quality school wholly concerned with fine art studies. However, artistically Cornwall was in a state of decline. In the previous year, 1975, three of the most prominent artists who had formed the group working in St Ives in the 1950s had died – Barbara Hepworth, Bryan Wynter and Roger Hilton. Others had gone elsewhere. One of these, Terry Frost, then living in Banbury, had taught with me at the University of Reading. I well remember him saying, in respect of art in Cornwall, 'Its all over, its all finished'. And so it seemed. When I arrived in Cornwall to take up my post in September 1976 much of the innovative energy that had characterised the 1950s was no longer present. However a few of the major artists were still working there, notably Patrick Heron, John Wells and Denis Mitchell. Terry Frost was soon to return.*

*Writing this in 2005 the situation has sadly changed. Of recent years a number of the most prominent artists connected with St Ives have died: Denis Mitchell in March 1993 aged 87, Patrick Heron in March 1999 aged 79, John Wells in July 2000 aged 93, Terry Frost in September 2003 aged 87, and Wilhelmina Barns Graham in January 2004 aged 91.

Falmouth School of Art had established good relations with artists in Cornwall. Barbara Hepworth had been an important supporter at an earlier and crucial period in the School's development. Patrick Heron and his wife Delia – then a Governor of the School – had given unstinted support over many years and in earlier times Peter Lanyon and Bryan Wynter had taught at the School.

In order to better understand the remarkable progress of modernism in St Ives that had occurred in the 1950s I conducted a series of interviews with those artists that still remained, including Patrick Heron, Denis Mitchell, John Wells and others. This research was eventually presented in two forms, as a book on the story of modern art in Cornwall entitled *Painting the Warmth of the Sun – Artists in Cornwall 1930–1975* (published in 1984) and a series of three films for Channel 4 Television shown in the same year and under the same title. Happily my book and the films coincided with other efforts to describe and evaluate the creative force of painting and sculpture in Cornwall in these earlier years. These lead to a considerable revival of interest in this period, to a definitive exhibition at the Tate Gallery in London in 1985 entitled *St Ives 1939–64*, and later to the building of the Tate St Ives, which was opened by the Prince of Wales in June 1993.

For me this was a transitional period. In Cornwall new images began to appear. Although still structural and formal and using strong primary colour, the work now had a new feeling for space. The subjects of my painting had also changed. The rivers of south-west Cornwall replaced my visits to the rugged landscape of North Wales. I began to make studies from the Falmouth Estuary, St Mawes, St Anthony, and Pendennis Head. I also continued to visit Wales, but less frequently. In the mid nineteen-seventies, at a time when my painting was in a state of change from formal abstraction to a type of figuration based on landscape, it was Cornwall that brought me back to landscape.

The use of the window as a subject in painting is a cubist device in which the picture becomes a window within a window. The exterior landscape is on one plane. The window, held by its frame and glazing bars, creates another plane, and the interior of the room is a third. These three planes give, in the words of Ben Nicholson 'a space in which the imagination can wander'. The window is a continuing theme in my painting.

One of the first of the 'Window' series is 'Window Zennor' 1977, based on a view from Eagles Nest, the home of the artist Patrick Heron, situated on the coast of the Penwith Peninsula, some 800 feet above sea level with an uninterrupted view to the west. In the evening the layered spread of cloud was coloured by the radiance of the setting sun and held by the rectangle of the window, a combination of the near and the immeasurably distant. We were staying temporarily in this house while our own in Falmouth was being repaired. The drawings and small paintings that I made there gave rise to a series under the general title 'In a Window'.

Living in Falmouth in a tall house overlooking the harbour provided subjects in the life of the river, the effects of light, the movement of water and the constant maritime activity of a busy port. The series 'In a Window' was based on a view from this house, the distant landscape of the port set within the framing of a Georgian window frame. In the foreground a plant with broad leaves created a third plane in the painting.

In 1985 I moved to Port Navas, a creek-side village on the Helford River. Here I was closer to the river and by boat I was able to explore the quiet inlets, the many wooded creeks and deep-water estuaries. These explorations have provided and continue to provide constant stimulation. My house overlooks the creek and a number of paintings have been done from the sitting room. The windows frame this view and give stability to a scene which is always in movement and infinitely varied.

Zennor Head March 16 87.

Window at Zennor 1977
Gouache

Window in Falmouth 1978
Pencil Drawing

In a Window, Evening Light 1980
Oil on canvas 129 x 102 cm

In a Window 1 1978
Oil on canvas 152 x 122 cm

Still Life in a Window 1, 1979
Oil on canvas 1Z x 102 cm

Falmouth River 1980
Oil on canvas

River and Trees 3, 1980
Gouache

Red Still Life, In a Window 1980
Screen Print 77 x 57 cm

Open Window 1985
Gouache 56 x 77 cm

River Rising 1987
Oil on canvas 102 x 122 cm

Window to the River 1987
Oil on canvas 92 x 152 cm

CHAPTER SEVEN
REALISM AND ABSTRACTION

It is clear from these notes that throughout my work abstraction and realism have gone hand in hand. From time to time one of these has been dominant but never wholly at the expense of the other. I feel that there is no need to choose. Ben Nicholson wrote 'Slightly more or less abstract for me is beside the point'. ('Notes on Abstract Art'. *Horizon* Vol IV no 22 1941).

During the 1970s my work took on a more abstract and structured form, as did that of many artists at this time. Since my early training as an architect I have retained an interest in architectural space, so the forms of architecture became a theme for investigation.

At about this time in the early 1970s the work of an exhibiting group called 'Systems', a collection of friends lead by the painter and constructivist Malcolm Hughes, interested me and I took part in their discussions. A characteristic of their method was that the process of making a work might be planned in an organised, often geometric way, but the final results were often surprising. I was sympathetic to this point of view, perhaps as an aspect of my own personality.

The paintings that I was making at that time were not made to a system or plan, their aim was exploration. Both chance and planned elements were used to examine the tensions that arise when a system which is under control meets uncontrolled action, an attempt to make planned elements interact unpredictably with random elements. If the result becomes predictable, the direction of the picture changes.

Willows 1972
Oil on canvas
Exhibited at University College, Aberysth

This period of total abstraction continued into the later 1970s. This was an important time because it allowed for experiment and discovery. The ingredients were simple, usually lozenge shapes or hexagons, but these are shapes that are suggestive of space. When repeated many times they can form a three-dimensional network.

A number of these experimental pieces were made while I was in the USA as a visiting Professor at Ohio State University. They were shown at the Hopkins Hall Gallery in May 1971 under the title 'Light Works'. In the catalogue to that exhibition I wrote:

My paintings are mainly about the places that are made for people to live in – their rooms and houses, the windows that they look out of, the pattern of roads and the city landscape, of high rise office and apartment buildings. However to release the energy of these familiar objects their form must be reduced to essentials and stripped of all that is arbitrary and unnecessary.

We live in a world of horizontals and verticals, but we see them as angled shapes. If, for instance, a cube is drawn as if seen from one corner, the result is a hexagon, made up of three diamond shapes. These inclined shapes have a special quality, because they lie flat on a canvas and direct the eye over it's surface and at the same time weave an illusion of three dimensional space. If they are held in a grid system, and allowed to take up their position and their colour by chance, they echo the complexities of the city landscape.

The comparison between two dimensional flatness and three dimensional form can be seen also by the use of projected light. When a network of cubes is shadowed upon a flat surface, the three dimensional shape becomes two dimensional. If the projected image moves, and alternately catches and releases painted shapes on the canvas, the result is a continuous interchange between two and three dimensional form.

The other main ingredient is of course colour. Colour is all pervading and convinces by its power and its certainty. On the flat surface we can create space between colours, an environment for the imagination. Many of these paintings use the primary colours, red, yellow, blue. The decision to paint an area in one of these colours or not to paint that area at all was often directed by chance – spinning a wheel or throwing of dice – thus the painting became a form of discovery rather than the pursuit of a fixed idea.

At the time that I came to Cornwall in 1976 I was working on a number of paintings that were to do with the mixture of colour in light. These had a strong theoretical basis. If, for example, a beam of red light is projected on to a screen and over it is projected an area of green light, a grey is produced which is lighter in tone than either of the two constituent colours. If light of another colour is added the mixture becomes lighter still, going towards white. The more light of whatever colour is added the lighter is the mixture. This is called 'the positive interaction of colour'. A number of my paintings were based on this phenomenon using paint on canvas together with projected light.

This increasing interest in colour and its relationship to space resulted in a major touring exhibition in 1975 called Colour, which brought together the work of ten contemporary abstract artists for whom colour was in differing ways a central preoccupation in their work. My own contribution to this exhibition was based on an investigation of the internal geometry of a building and I produced a series of paintings entitled 'Taliesin' after the home and studio of Frank Lloyd Wright in Arizona: a wizardry of desert rock, rough sawn planks, canvas screens and shutters, the sun passes through the structure and dissolves out the colour and form. This was also related to the form of a recently completed studio built for myself in Reading in 1974, and the paintings used the elements of the building, the post and lintel, the divisions of space made by the timber frame and sloping roof.

Some of the paintings were very large, averaging eight feet and they were mostly to do with the interaction of colour. Often the choice of colour was decided by chance on the turn of a dice. I would set up a grid so that theoretically a colour could be placed on any part it. Whether the colour was yellow, blue, green or red or whether no colour was added depended on how the dice fell. This was an experiment which created new situations in painting for me. However, although in the past I have been interested in colour theory, there are no theories that really work, you have just got to do it and test the results. Now my colour is mostly intuitive, you can put any two colours together but it's what you do with them that counts, the way they contain by their shape, the way they interact with other colours around them.

As an alternative to landscape I have also often used still life as a subject. The forms that I use are simple, a few well-known jugs, bottles, mugs and beakers on a table. Their familiar contours set up a resonance with each other and they are instantly familiar by their outline. The paintings often contain a window with a simplified river landscape behind. This combination of realism and abstraction is the area in which I feel most at home.

Light Piece 1971
Screen Print

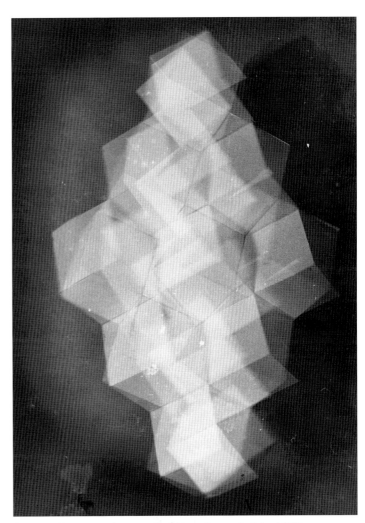

Rotating Structure photographed in stroboscopic light 1970

Spin 1971
Acrylic on canvas   152 x 244 cm

The Exhibition 'Light Works' 1971

Taliesin 1976
Oil on masonite 177 x 152 cm

Primary 3, 1977
Oil on canvas 122 x 122 cm

Three times Three 1978
Oil on canvas 197 x 197 cm

Terry's Birthday 1988
Oil on canvas 61 x 66

Yellow Jug 1990
Gouache 23 x 21 cm

Still Life with Fountain 1990
Gouache 52 x 72 cm

Blue Jug and Oysters 1991
Oil on canvas 66 x 51 cm

CHAPTER EIGHT

OTHER PLACES

Although the Helford has been a continuing theme in my painting a great deal has been done in other countries, as far distant as the United States, Australia, Dubai and Oman, Guernsey, Venice and other parts of Italy and France. When staying in a new country, a period of drawing has its own special reward and provides an additional level of understanding. I look for the unfamiliar, an unexpected grouping of buildings or a particular quality of light. To understand this experience it is necessary to work directly from nature and it is only later that strongly structured or abstract means are possible. To impose a stylistic form upon such discoveries would be to falsify their impact and to destroy the mystery of their settings. The drawings and studies made on these overseas visits, some of them of considerable duration, have provided a background to my work over many years.

The United States

New opportunities often require new beginnings. This was the case when, in 1971, I became visiting exchange Professor at Ohio State University, Columbus. With a minimum of teaching the University gave me the use of a large studio and the opportunity to travel in the United States. The scale of my own work increased and I was able to make a new investigation into space, initially disciplined by geometry. The forms that I used, complex grids of rectangles and diamond shapes, were affected by the street patterns of the American cities. This was also an opportunity to see the work of the American artists and to get to know some of them. I was able to make several visits to New York and to take an extended trip with my family to the far West including California, Arizona and New Mexico. The vastness of America seemed to be in accord with the new painting that was being produced there and my own work was affected by this sense of scale and freedom.

To quote from a statement that I made in 1971:

The formal paintings are not made to a system or plan, the aim and object is exploration. If the result becomes predictable the direction of the picture changes. Both chance and planned elements are used to explore the tensions that arise when a system that is under control requires uncontrolled action – the known and the unknown. An attempt to go beyond logic.

These large paintings were shown in several exhibitions in the United States and later in England and Wales.

Charleston

A further visit to the United States in 1983, for a year, was to Charleston, South Carolina. I had many powerful impressions of the South and found subjects in the humid atmosphere of the plantations and the flat lands of the coast with their marshes and palmetto forests. I also made drawings and paintings of the fine buildings of historic Charleston and the grandeur of the Blue Ridge Mountains of North Carolina.

Mexico

At the end of the teaching term at the College of Charleston my wife and I made an extended visit to Mexico. Three months were spent travelling around that extraordinary country, starting in Mexico City and moving on south and east to Oaxaca, the Yucatan peninsular and the Chiapas area, visiting most of the principal archaeological sites such as Uxmal, Chichen Itza and Palenque.

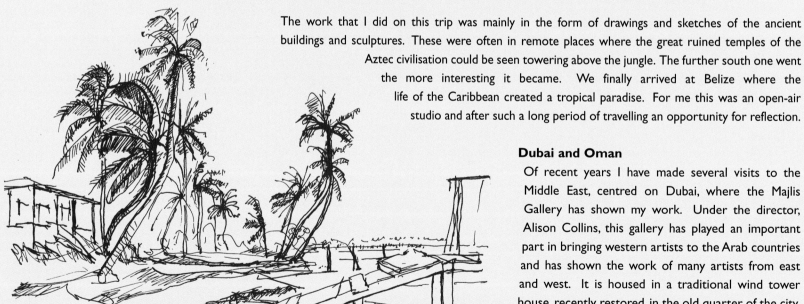

The work that I did on this trip was mainly in the form of drawings and sketches of the ancient buildings and sculptures. These were often in remote places where the great ruined temples of the Aztec civilisation could be seen towering above the jungle. The further south one went the more interesting it became. We finally arrived at Belize where the life of the Caribbean created a tropical paradise. For me this was an open-air studio and after such a long period of travelling an opportunity for reflection.

Dubai and Oman

Of recent years I have made several visits to the Middle East, centred on Dubai, where the Majlis Gallery has shown my work. Under the director, Alison Collins, this gallery has played an important part in bringing western artists to the Arab countries and has shown the work of many artists from east and west. It is housed in a traditional wind tower house, recently restored, in the old quarter of the city.

San Pedro.
Ambergris Cay. 26 July 84

My own visits to Dubai date from 1996 when I went as a guest of the gallery and was also able to visit and exhibit my work in Oman and other Arab Emirate countries. My subjects included the mix of architecture, old and new, in the modern cities of Arabia and the ferocious mountain landscape of the Hajar desert to the east. I tried to understand these places in their own terms and to see these arid terrains with their unusual light, so different from Cornwall.

Australia

A further extended visit, in 1999, was to the west coast of Australia. I had gone there principally to give a series of lectures to the Australian Decorative and Fine Arts Societies which are in the principal cities of the east coast, but I was also invited to have an exhibition on the western coast of Australia at Gallery East in Fremantle. In order to prepare for this, I made a preliminary journey to Western Australia and travelled by car along the south-western coast of the continent, stopping to record my impressions. The repetitive sameness of the landscape and its unfamiliarity deserved a much longer study

On another occasion in 1992 I was able to visit Western Samoa in the south Pacific, and to spend several weeks in the exotic splendour of this island paradise. The luxuriant vegetation and the settled life of the villages around the coast were in vivid contrast to the bustling cities of Australia.

Guernsey

Guernsey is not large but it is very varied. To the north and the west of the island are long outcrop rocks and in the north are deep inlets and bays with projecting headlands. A sombre addition is the German gun emplacements from the Second World War.

I first visited Guernsey in 1998 in order to paint an exhibition for the Coach House Gallery. I produced a large number of drawings and watercolours, many of which were translated into larger scale works. Drawing helped me to understand the qualities of an unfamiliar landscape, although in many ways this is not dissimilar to Cornwall.

One of the paintings of Guernsey was done in a place that I particularly like called Saint's Bay, which is in the south of the island. I was painting on the cliff overlooking this deep bay when I heard two ladies pass above me. I did not even look around to see who they were, but I heard one of them say 'There is a painter working down there'. Her companion replied 'Oh yes, did you know that Renoir painted this bay?' Later I found out that Renoir had painted about 30 pictures in that partic-ular area. I felt that I was in very good company.

Blue Ridge Mountains, North Carolina 1983
Gouache

4 Chapel Street, Charleston. South Carolina 1984
Pencil and ink

The Pyramids, Tula, Mexico 1984
Ink drawing

Temple of the Moon, Teotihuacan 1985
Gouache

Coral Reef, Belize 1984
Watercolour 43 x 42 cm

Banana Tree, Western Samoa 1992
Watercolour

Arabian Courtyard 1997
Gouache 71 x51 cm

Hajar Mountains, Oman 1996
Watercolour 34 x 53 cm

On the Road to Kalgoorlie, Western Australia, 1999
Gouache 35 x 52 cm

Tuart Forest, Western Australia 2, 1999
Watercolour 53 x 73 cm

Saint's Bay, Guernsey 1998
Watercolour 72 x 63 cm

CHAPTER NINE

EARLY INFLUENCES

After leaving the Slade in 1956 two years were spent painting in Italy and France. On returning to London it was clear that to exist entirely on painting in the late 1950s was beyond my expectations. In 1959 I was offered the post of assistant Director of the Welsh Arts Council, responsible for the visual arts programme for Wales. This allowed me to explore many parts of the Principality, to become familiar with its coast and mountains and to meet and make friends with many people involved in various artistic enterprises. It was a time of expansion and development in the arts and an opportunity to initiate programmes for artists in Wales which later found fruition.

The wild landscape of the places in which I have lived has been a recurring subject for my work. In the drawings that I did at this time, realism, that is the direct translation of the scene as one sees it, is most in evidence. The more dramatic the landscape the less one wishes to change it. Nevertheless in all my work there is an attempt, not always conscious, but evident, to reduce the subjects to its components in order to examine it better.

I had visited the mountains of North Wales on climbing and walking expeditions in the early 1950s and the rugged strength of the Snowdon range was impressive. In the process of drawing a form is found which is true to the landscape and to the artist's feelings for it. The abrasive character of the landscape, hills and rocks, cloud and the effects of weather and the familiarity of certain places acted as a continued stimulus. In an exhibition catalogue of this time I described my desire 'to parallel the landscape rather than to describe it'.

Based in Cardiff and living in the small village of Rhiwsaeson near Llantrisant my job took me to many parts of Wales and I came to know the cliffs and beaches of Pembrokeshire as well as the dramatic landscape of Snowdonia that I had earlier explored. These landscape paintings formed an important part of my first exhibition at the Howard Roberts Gallery in Cardiff. This feeling for the wild places of Wales have continued to play an important part in my work since that time.

Although architecture was no longer my practice I remained interested in architectural space and design. In the early 1960s this found expression in a series of paintings based on the rebuilding of an old cottage where we lived in Rhiwsaeson. The texture and the materials of the old building were opposed by the straight lines and sharp angles of newly built work, the elements of the structure, post and beam, the angled roof trusses and horizontal rafters. In a series of large paintings these elements took on their own role as part of an abstract composition.

Cader Idris

In 1963 I left the Welsh Arts Council to take up a teaching post at the University of Reading but my connection with Wales continued. The use of a cottage in the Prescelly Hills in Pembrokeshire brought close contact with the rough windswept landscape and gave me a subject that was lacking in the more urban environment of Berkshire. Repeated visits to the Snowdonia area of North Wales centred on and around Dolgellau gave access to Cader Idris, this sculptural mountain became a frequent subject for large watercolours,

There are close parallels between the land and people of Cornwall and of Wales, each has kept its Celtic identity and they share a magic of coast, moor and mountain and the privacy of their wild places. Whilst Cornwall has been my home for many years I have kept my connection with the University of Wales through regular visits and as examiner in art at the University of Wales, Aberystwyth. An important group of work done around Cader Idris has been a result of this continuing collaboration.

Reading

In 1963 Claude Rogers who had been my tutor at the Slade School and recently appointed as Professor of Fine Art at Reading University, asked me to join him there. This was a time of expansion in the University, new posts were created and new teaching methods were explored. For a time I worked with students on an introductory course in Fine Art together with Terry Frost and Rita Donagh, following teaching ideas that had been developed by Victor Pasmore and Richard Hamilton, then working in other parts of the country.

For myself the 1970s was a time of experiment. The swing between architectural ideas and those derived from landscape continued. I became particularly interested in the architecture of the Baroque period in Rome. Drawings of the churches such as Santa Maria della Pace, San Carlino and Bernini's San Andrea al Quirinale explored the free flow of space and the spectator involvement that is so evident in these buildings. I used the hexagonal ceiling coffers as a motif. These shapes can be read as three-dimensional views of a cube and may manipulate space to suggest movement.

San Andrea al Quirinale,
Rome 1966

Mountain Landscape 1957
Ink drawing

Cader Idris Three Peaks 1963
Ink drawing 13 x 23 cm

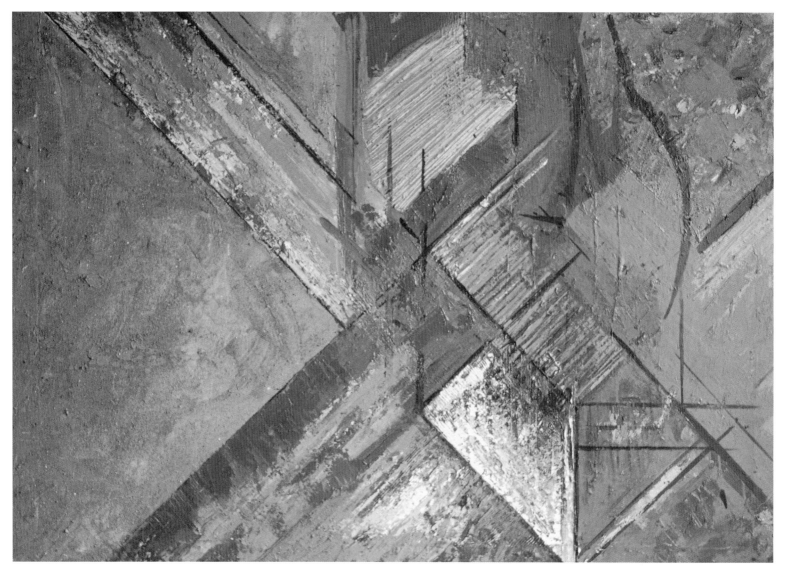

The Cottage 1961
Oil on canvas

Interior of a Room 1964
Oil on canvas 183 x 133 cm

Red Landscape 1964
Oil on canvas 76 x 102 x cm

Pembrokeshire Coast 1966
Gouache

S Maria della Pace, Rome 1966
Gouache 36 x 66 cm

CHAPTER TEN
TRAINING AND TRAVEL

Art at school was taught, as in many Grammar Schools of the period, as a partly optional subject, not of great academic importance. I was particularly fortunate in having as my art teacher, Nathaniel Parker, brother to the well known film actor Cecil Parker. He gave gentle encouragement, with the minimum of interference, and the pupils were naturally assisted to find their own direction.

Following a period in the RAF, my art training proper began at Manchester School of Art in the early 1950s. This was a broadly based course, which offered the opportunity to explore a wide range of two and three dimensional skills. I had been apprenticed to a Manchester architect and worked for a time as an architectural draughtsman and as a consequence I initially enrolled for a course in architecture.

Manchester School of Art was a fairly quiet, easy-going sort of place; it gave me time to find a direction and to experiment and it inculcated a certain discipline of work. The introductory year was a joint course for potential artists and architects. I joined it with the intention of going towards architecture and followed the first year course which consisted of a wide range of subjects such as building design and building construction as well as painting, drawing and general design work. After a year I decided to change my course towards Fine Art, which seemed to offer more imaginative and expressive possibilities.

My time at Manchester was not unpleasant but I did not think I was experiencing something extraordinary. The most important thing that happened to me at that time was meeting L S Lowry, the only professional artist I got to know at Manchester, and forming a friendship which continued in later years. He was also a help and support to many of the students by accepting the Presidency of the 'Northern Young Artists' an exhibiting society that I helped to form in Manchester.

I went to the Slade School in London in 1953 as a postgraduate student. The move from Manchester to the Slade was a revelation. It was enormously helpful to me in all sorts of directions and gave me the opportunity to work with people who were very serious about what they were doing and who did it very well.

It was a flourishing period; William Coldstream had come three years before as Slade Professor and he had made many changes but they were very subtle. Although I did not recognise it at the time, the School was undergoing a major revival. There was a very broad basis to the teaching; instruction was centred upon drawing and painting from the model, but this was by no means prescriptive or limiting. Although we were aware of Coldstream's painting method of comparative measurement, there was no pressure to follow his example.

At that time the Slade was at the centre of advanced art activity in Britain. Coldstream had brought in a large number of well known artists as part-time teachers, so you met just about everybody in the contemporary art world. Several of the friends of Coldstream's earlier years were members of staff, including Claude Rogers and William Townsend who had worked with him at the Euston Road School in the late 1930s. The main form of teaching was a discussion of work with your tutor; this occurred once a month and my tutor was Claude Rogers. A further interest of mine was in stage design under the painter and designer Robert Medley, and I was able to meet and to work with leading theatrical producers who set student projects.

Even more important to me, the Slade provided the opportunity to meet and to have discussions with many of the leading British artists of the time such as Ceri Richards, Patrick Heron, John Piper, Henry Moore and others. A whole range of people came in as tutorial visitors – everybody who you could reasonably wish for, even some French artists used to visit. The presence of these remarkable people opened up a whole lot of directions. If you did not get something from this rich mixture the problem was with you. To be part of this intellectual powerhouse was a memorable if sometimes painful experience. I remember describing the Slade at that time as a mixture of conservatory and monastery .

This was a time of change in the directions of British Art. The stages of that change can be measured in the work of Victor Pasmore as he moved through forms of poetic realism based on French painting, to various stages of formal abstraction. Artists and students alike watched this process with close attention. In several tutorials that I had with him he talked of modern painting as a new thing. He stressed the point that between a recording made in a traditional way and what he termed 'new art' there was a river that must be crossed and the far side was a different country. I particularly remember his comments on a small painting of a river which he liked because it was painted from the inside rather than a visual construction of something seen.

Travel

I have always felt that the most rewarding and productive opportunities lay in travel. The exploration of different and unfamiliar cultures, of learning new languages and of seeing one's own country from a different perspective, all of these seemed a natural extension of learning. Added to this was the expansion in art that was occurring world wide.

The offer of a third post-graduate year at the Slade was particularly welcome for it opened up new horizons and brought the opportunity for me to travel and to live abroad. During the summer vacation of 1955 I made the first of a series of visits to Italy that have continued since that time. I came to know particularly the area of the Marche, the old Papal provinces to the east of Rome. With friends from the Slade over several summers we were centred on the provincial town of Recanati and the Italian landscape became a subject for my work at that time. Italy shares with Cornwall an intensity of brilliant light, the movement of its rocky landscape, hill and valley, and the pattern of ancient fields.

My knowledge of Italy developed further when I was awarded a scholarship to the British School in Rome and I was able to spend a year in that city, living at the British School in the Valle Julia. I was also able to travel extensively throughout the country. In addition to painting and drawing, mostly from landscape subjects, I made many drawings of the buildings of Italy. To gain a little extra money I worked as a draughtsman for the Director of the School on his studies of the Etruscan road network of Central Italy. This meant visiting some of the remote sites of ancient Etruscan cities in order to prepare drawings and photographs. I also worked briefly for the Italian architect Bruno Zevi.

This period of living abroad continued with a year in France on a French Government Scholarship. During this time I married Patricia (Carrick) and we lived for a time in Paris, then on the Mediterranean coast at Antibes and later in Biot. During this period of two years I came to know in more detail the example of contemporary European art and my own work took on more direct and objective forms of realist painting.

The examples that I was looking at this time were the French painters from Cézanne onwards. France still seemed to be the centre of the artistic universe but this situation was soon to change. In January 1956 the Tate Gallery, London, put on an exhibition entitled 'Modern Art in the United States' which was a selection from the collections of the Museum of Modern Art, New York. The last

Three palm trees from the terrace of 28 Rue des Bains.

Pensione
Seguso
Zattere

132

part of this large exhibition was a group of twenty-seven paintings exhibited as 'Contemporary Abstract Art' and including such artists as Philip Guston, Franz Kline, Willem de Kooning, Robert Motherwell and Jackson Pollock. I had seen this exhibition shortly before I had left for Italy and I had found the experience unsettling, although I had recognised the importance of this work. During the two years in which I was out of England the whole of the artistic scene had altered and the new focus of attention became the United States and New York in particular.

Because of my absence from London I believe that I was less affected than some of my contemporaries by the new American painting but the scale of these paintings and the freedom to find abstract form from the visual world can be seen in a number of my paintings in subsequent years, such as 'Red Landscape'. This is an analogy of landscape in which the sweep of a brush and the spread of paint can take on the forms of landscape without being dependent upon detailed description. Another even more gestural and totally abstract is 'Yellow and Two Reds', both are dated 1964.

My first visit to Cornwall was made in the summer of 1954 whilst I was still a student at the Slade. I was here for a long summer staying in Falmouth, Mevagissey, Gorran Haven and other places. When the friend I was travelling with had to return, I decided to stay and got a job at the Budock Vean Hotel, on the Helford River as a waiter and part-time caddy on the golf course. I was one of the young itinerant staff that picked up summer jobs and tried to exist through the winter. One young waiter had his life already set on crime. He showed me his most precious possession, which was a gun, loaded and ready for use. Another young waitress dreamt through her days and claimed to be writing the great novel of social life in England.

When the time came eventually to depart I packed my rucksack and walked to the gates of the hotel hoping for a lift into Falmouth. I soon got one from a friendly chap driving a Morris Eight. As we talked in the car he asked me if I was in a hurry, clearly I was not. He suggested I might like to go sailing, which I gladly accepted. At the end of a perfect day sailing in the Carrick Roads we came back to his moorings in Mylor and when he left the boat he said that I could sleep on board. I woke to a perfect morning and rowed ashore to find something to eat for breakfast. A farm worker leading a horse-drawn cart said that I could get milk and bread from his farm. This memorable day ended with my doing two drawings of his boat, one of which I sent back to this friendly individual. From that time I had a persistent memory of Cornwall as a perfect place (illustrated by 'Two Boys Swimming' 1954, see page 138). This early experience offered much of what ultimately came to be so important to me – an introduction to that part of Cornwall dominated by the Fal and the Helford Rivers which became the basis of my painting.

Northern Landscape *1954*
Gouache 15 x 31 cm

L S Lowry and Tom Cross study some of the Paintings of the Northern Young Artists Exhibition.
Oldham Art Gallery, September 1953

Recanati 4, 1953
Gouache 38 x 46 cm

Massignano – Landscape in the Marche 1, 1956
Oil on canvas 61 x 66 cm

Tree in Rome 1957
Oil on canvas

Balcony and Cactus. Biot, 1958
Oil on canvas 76 x 60cm

Two Boys Swimming, 1954
Oil on canvas

CHRONOLOGY

Born in Manchester. Educated at St Bede's RC College, Manchester. On leaving school was apprenticed to the architects Thomas Worthington & Son in Manchester.

1949–53
Trained at Manchester School of Art where he was awarded the Proctor Scholarship, the Plummer Scholarship, the Silver Medal for Painting of the Royal Manchester Institution and gained the National Diploma in Design. Founder Member of the Northern Young Artists Association. He first met L S Lowry when he approached him on behalf of the Association to become its President. They remained friends until Lowry's death in 1976.

1953–56
Attended the Slade School of Art, University of London. President of the Slade Society. Awarded the Robert Stanbury Post-Graduate Scholarship. Gained the Diploma in Fine Art (London).

1956–58
Awarded the Abbey Minor Scholarship. Worked at the British School in Rome and travelled in northern Italy. Awarded a French Government scholarship and worked for a year in Paris and the South of France.

1957
Married Patricia Carrick. Son David born in 1961.

1959
Moved to Wales on his appointment as Assistant Director of the Welsh Arts Council, based in Cardiff.

1963
Lecturer in Fine Art at the University of Reading. Senior Lecturer 1969–1976.

1970–1
Visiting Professor for six months at Ohio State University, Columbus, USA.

1976
Appointed Principal of Falmouth School of Art where he remained until 1987. Elected Member of the Penwith Society of Artists, St Ives. Later Chairman of the Penwith Galleries Ltd.

1978
Elected Member of the London Group.

1983–4
Visiting Professor at the Simons Centre for the Arts, College of Charleston, South Carolina, USA.

1989–94
External Examiner in Art and in Art History, the University of Wales, Aberystwyth and at the University of Exeter.

1989–1994
Lecturer in Continuing Education. University of Exeter.

1998–2000
Examiner in Fine Art to the Dublin Institute of Technology

1994–2003
Lecturer for the National Association of Decorative and Fine Art Societies (NADFAS)

Exhibitions

1955: Gimpel Fils, London

1959: 'Young Contemporary Painters', University of Nottingham

CHRONOLOGY

1961: Ashgate Gallery, Farnham *

1963: Howard Roberts Gallery, Cardiff *

1963: Everyman Theatre, Cardiff *

1963: Dillwyn Gallery, Swansea *

1965: 'Four Painters and Two Sculptors', Bangor Art Gallery. John Moore's Exhibition, Walker Art Gallery, Liverpool.

1966: Playhouse Theatre, Oxford *

1967: London Group. 'The Roman Baroque', photographic exhibition at Chelsea School of Art.

1968: Arranged and exhibited in 'Twelve Artists', Reading Museum.
'Pembrokeshire Landscape', Playhouse Theatre, Oxford *
'Paintings and Constructions', Architectural Assoc. London *

1969: 'Recent Paintings by Tom Cross', Sussex University Arts Centre *
'On Paper – an Exhibition of Recent Graphic Work', Reading Museum & Art Gallery, Ikon Gallery, Birmingham, Manchester College of Advanced Education and Birmingham College of Art. 'Structural Growth in Natural Form', Whitechapel Gallery, London

1970: 'Light Works, Paintings and Prints', AIA Gallery, London WC2.
'Two Painters and a Sculptor', Manchester

1971: 'Light Works – Paintings and Graphics by Tom Cross', Hopkins Hall Gallery, Ohio State University, Columbus, USA *

1972–1973: 'Light Works' shown at the University of Wales, Aberystwyth, the Welsh Arts Council Gallery, Cardiff, Reading Museum and Art Gallery and the Durham Light Infantry Gallery, Durham.

1975–1976: 'Colour', arranged and exhibited, toured by Southern Arts to Southampton, Winchester, Worthing, Portsmouth, Bracknell, Salisbury and Falmouth

141

1976: Regular exhibitor at the Penwith Society of Artists, St Ives from this date.

1977: Wills Lane Gallery, St Ives.

1978: London Group, Gulbenkian Galleries, Royal College of Art, London. A regular exhibitor with the London Group from this date.
'Recent Paintings', the Penwith Gallery, St Ives with Breon O'Casey

1979: 'Prints and Etchings by Invited Artists', Penwith Gallery, St Ives,

1980: 'Art in the Making', King Street Gallery, Bristol, the Victoria Art Gallery, Bath, and the Brewhouse Theatre, Taunton,

1981: 'Paintings from Cornwall', Montpelier Studio Gallery, London *

1984: 'A River and Some Landscapes', William Halsey Gallery, Charleston, USA*
'Artists of Fame and Promise', Montpelier Studio Gallery, London

1985: 'The St Ives Tradition', Montpelier Studio Gallery, London

1986: 'Ocean Landscapes', Jan Going Gallery, Charleston, South Carolina, USA*
'Cornish Connections', 3D Gallery, Bristol

1987: Grenville Gibbs Corporate Art, London

1989: 'Paintings of Cornwall', Austin Desmond Fine Art, London* Albany Gallery, Cardiff.

1989–1990: 'The Northem Scene', touring exhibition

1990: Pelter Sands Gallery Bristol - 3 man show.

1992: 'A Centenary Exhibition', University of Reading.
'Artists from Cornwall', Royal West of England Academy. Royal West of England Academy, Autumn Exhibition
'Italy and Cornwall – Paintings by Tom Cross', Stephen Bartley Gallery, London

CHRONOLOGY

1993: 'Homage to Claude Rogers', Royal West of England Academy.
'Summer Exhibition', Montpelier Studio Gallery, London
'Italian Paintings', Richard Philp Gallery, London *

1994: 'The Art of the Chelsea Arts Club', Chelsea Town Hall.

1995–1996: 'Tom Cross – Paintings of Cornwall and Wales'. The University of Wales, School of Art Gallery, Aberystwyth. The University of Birmingham, the Goldmark Gallery, Rutland, and the Penwith Gallery, St Ives.*

1997: 'The New Orientalists' The Cultural Centre, Abhu Dhabi and the Majlis Gallery, Dubai. One-man exhibition at the Residence of the British Ambassador, Muscat, the Sultanate of Oman. *

1998: 'Tom Cross Paintings', The Coach-house Gallery, Guernsey, Channel Isles. *

1999: 'Visits to Wales', Christopher Hall, Bob Brown & Tom Cross, Royal Cambrian Academy, Conwy, North Wales.

1999: 'Paintings of Comwall and Australia' at Gallery East, Fremantle, Western Australia. *
The First Ten Years', the Majlis Gallery, Dubai.

2000: 'Recent Paintings' at the Penwith Gallery, St Ives, Cornwall. *

2002: 'Landmarks of Arabia', the Majlis Gallery, Dubai.
Commissioned to paint a mural for a swimming pool at 11 Eaton Square, London.

2003: 'Paintings of the Helford River', The Garden Gallery, Trebah, Cornwall*.
'Paintings of Venice', the Chelsea Arts Club, London*

* = One man show

Public Collections

The University of Wales Aberystwyth, Glamorgan Education Authority, Leicestershire Education Authority, Walker Art Gallery, Liverpool, Contemporary Art Society, London, Whitworth Art Gallery, University of Manchester, Ohio State University, Reading Borough Council, University of Reading, Salford City Art Gallery, Southern Arts, University of Sussex, Brighton, Arts Council for Wales, Contemporary Art Society for Wales, IBM. The British Embassy, Oman, German Embassy, Abhu Dhabi, Private Collections in Europe, Australia, Dubai, North and South America.

Publications

How Impressionism Began, Welsh Arts Council for the National Museum of Wales, Cardiff 1960
Ceri Richards, The Royal National Eisteddfod of Wales, Cardiff 1961
Joseph Herman, The Royal National Eisteddfod of Wales, Llanelli 1962
British Art and the Modern Movement, The National Museum of Wales, Cardiff 1962.
Graham Sutherland – Drawings of Wales, Welsh Arts Council, Cardiff 1963.
Two Painters: Brenda Chamberlain and Ernest Zobole, Welsh Arts Council, Cardiff 1963.
John Piper in Wales, Welsh Arts Council, Cardiff 1964.
The Slade Tradition, Fine Art Society, London 1971.
Colour, Exhibition and Catalogue, Southern Arts, 1976.
Art in the Making, Exhibition catalogue for South West Arts
Painting the Warmth of the Sun – St Ives Artists 1930-1975, Alison Hodge, Penzance, Lutterworth Press, Cambridge 1984, Halsgrove 1995.
Painting the Warmth of the Sun, Script for three one-hour television programmes based on the book, Television South West for Channel 4, 1984
Artists and Bohemians, 100 years with the Chelsea Arts Club, Quiller Press, London 1992
Artists from Cornwall, Introduction to exhibition catalogue, Royal West of England Academy 1992
The Shining Sands, Artist in Newlyn and St Ives 1880-1930, Westcountry Books, Tiverton and Lutterworth Press, Cambridge 1994
The Artists of St Ives for NADFAS NEWS, Autumn/Winter 1995
Orientalism 1997. Introduction to the Catalogue for the New Orientalist Exhibition at the Majlis Gallery, Dubai.
The Artists of Newlyn, entry for the *New Dictionary of National Biography*.
Catching the Wave – Contemporary Art and Artists in Cornwall from 1975 to the Present, Halsgrove November 2002.